Ants in His Pants

Absurdities and Realities of Special Education

Cartoons by Michael F. Giangreco
Illustrations by Kevin Ruelle

Peytral Publications, Inc.
Minnetonka, MN 55345
952-949-8707

Publisher's Cataloging-in-Publication
(Provided by Quality Books, Inc.)

Giangreco, Michael F., 1956-
     Ants in his pants : absurdities and realities of special
education / Michael F. Giangreco. -- 1st ed.
          p. cm.
          ISBN: 1-890455-42-3

     1. Special education--United States--Humor.
  2. Mainstreaming in education--United States--Humor.
  3. Handicapped children--Education--United States--Humor.
  4. Home and school--United States--Humor.   I. Title.

LA23.G53 1998   371.9'0207
                                                        QBI98-613

Library of Congress Catalog Number 98-066391

Cartoon illustrations by Kevin Ruelle
Printed in the United States of America

Peytral Publications, Inc.
PO Box 1162
Minnetonka, MN 55345
Toll free - 1-877- Peytral
www.peytral.com

Contents

About the Author

Michael F. Giangreco, Ph.D., is a Research Associate Professor at the University of Vermont in the Department of Education. He has over twenty years experience working in the field of special education in a variety of capacities such as camp counselor, community residence counselor, special education teacher, special education coordinator, educational consultant, university teacher, and researcher. After 15 years of writing more traditional research studies, book chapters, and books, this is Michael's first effort to write cartoons. Although he will continue his scholarly pursuits, he plans to infuse more humor into his work and find creative ways to share information about the serious issues facing people with disabilities, their families, teachers, and service providers.

About the Illustrator

Kevin Ruelle has been an illustrator in Vermont for nineteen years. Cartoons are just one of the many applications for illustration that Kevin uses in his work. He runs a commercial art business, Ruelle Design and Illustration, located in Williston, Vermont. He produces all forms of visual communication and multimedia projects. Kevin lives with his wife Neidi and their four children in West Bolton, Vermont.

Ants in His Pants

A Word from the Author

The noted psychologist, Abraham Maslow, reminded us that we should "Laugh at what we hold sacred, and still hold it sacred." With that sentiment in mind, I present you with *Ants in His Pants: Absurdities and Realities of Special Education.* This set of cartoons is about some of the serious issues of special education, but pokes fun at what we (people in the field) do. The idea for a book of cartoons had been incubating in my mind for a few years before I finally spurred myself to action. My original cartoon drawings confirmed what I suspected all along, that I am "Severely Art-Impaired." So I took my primitive, stick-figure drawings to Kevin Ruelle. He was known to me primarily as a basketball-playing buddy, rumored to be a terror in barn hockey, and father of one of my son's middle school classmates. Kevin also happens to be a gifted artist who operates his own design and illustration company. I showed him my cartoons and he agreed to help bring them to life by transforming my drawings with his artistic talent. I wish every task I did was as synergistic as it was working with Kevin on this project -- it has been a real pleasure.

As I shared my early work with friends and colleagues I was encouraged by their laughter and positive responses. I was also challenged by their concerns that some people might be offended by the content that, for some, might hit a little too close to home. I decided to take the chance that people in our field had a sufficient sense of humor to reflect on the satirical aspects of these cartoons, see the humor in them, and use them to promote better schooling. People also expressed concerns that my cartoons could be misused to promote practices that are the antithesis of what I have worked for my entire professional career. Just so there is no misunderstanding about what I, and these cartoons, stand for, I have listed here some of my beliefs related to the cartoon content.

- Individuals with disabilities are still woefully undervalued in our society.

- We waste too many of our resources testing, sorting, and labeling people, usually so we can justify serving, separating, or excluding them.

- The general education classroom (with individually appropriate supports) should be the first placement option for children with disabilities; separate special education schools and classes continue to be unnecessarily overused.

- Inclusive education is desirable, therefore our efforts should be geared toward finding ways that it can work effectively for increasing numbers of students.

- People of all ages, with and without disabilities, have much to learn from each other.

- Collaborative teamwork is an important element of quality education.

- Families are the cornerstone of ongoing educational planning.

- Establishing a partnership between families and school personnel is vital to quality education.

- Families and professionals should work together to increase effective consumerism by families regarding educational services.

- Competent general educators can effectively teach students with disabilities when provided with appropriate supports.

- Special educators and related service providers (e.g., physical therapists, occupational therapists, speech/language pathologists, school psychologists) can, and do, make important contributions for many students with special educational needs.

- Paraprofessionals are playing an increasingly prominent role in the education of students with disabilities. These hard-working folks typically are underpaid, undertrained, and undersupervised. Too often this means that they inappropriately become the de facto teacher for students with the most complex and challenging educational needs.

- The IEP (Individual Education Plan) can be a powerful and useful tool to facilitate quality education for students with disabilities. Unfortunately, too often it is misused.

- At the heart of a quality education are the relationships among the members of the educational community, the quality of the curriculum, and the integrity of the instruction. We must attend to all three components if we hope to assist students in experiencing valued life outcomes.

So as you read the cartoons, keep in mind that they are meant to encourage better educational practices by considering various absurdities of some current practices. We hope they stimulate you to think about things differently and that you find creative ways to use them in your own efforts to improve education. We also hope that some of these cartoons make you smile and laugh because we sure could use more of that in education.

Enjoy!

Michael F. Giangreco

Acknowledgments

So many people inspired and encouraged me throughout this project. Thanks to my colleagues and friends around the country who inspired some of these cartoons: Doug Biklen, Mary Beth Doyle, Alan Gartner, Michael Hock, Robert Holland, Adelle Keegan, Norman Kunc, Dorothy Kerzner Lipsky, Mara Sapon-Shevin, Michele Sarkis, Peg Smith, Jacque Thousand, Rich Villa, and staff at the Institute on Disability at the University of New Hampshire. At the University of Vermont I received great encouragement from many of my colleagues, especially Michael Hock, Jane Ross-Allen, Susan Edelman, Ruth Dennis, and Chigee Cloninger. My greatest encouragement came from my fun and funny family, my wife Mary Beth Doyle and my two children, Melanie and Dan.

RECENT ARCHEOLOGICAL EVIDENCE
SUGGESTS THAT SPECIAL SCHOOLS
HAVE BEEN AROUND LONGER THAN
WE ONCE THOUGHT.

REPTILIAN RESPONSES TO DIVERSITY

LITTLE-KNOWN SPECIAL
EDUCATION HISTORY.

IGNORING THE NEED FOR
INCLUSIVE EDUCATION
DOESN'T MAKE IT GO AWAY.

ONE OF THE MANY PRACTICAL LIMITATIONS OF HOMOGENEOUS GROUPING.

MRS. BLUE IS WOEFULLY UNACCUSTOMED
TO GOOD NEWS.

AFTER WEEKS OF UNDERCOVER WORK, FRED
VERIFIES THAT SOMETIMES
NUMBERS DO LIE!

"PAROLE APPROACH"
TO SCHOOL INCLUSION

ROY HAS BEEN SITTING ON THE FENCE
FOR SO LONG THAT HE'S FORGOTTEN HOW
TO FORM HIS OWN OPINION.

ADMINISTRATION AT MISDEMEANOR
MIDDLE SCHOOL CONTINUES TO CONSIDER
THEMSELVES ABOVE THE LAW.

EXCLUSION + EXCUSES = "EXCLUSES"

COMMON REASONS FOR AVOIDING INCLUSIVE EDUCATION.

DESPITE THE BIO-ETHICAL CONTROVERSIES MAGGIE FAVORS HUMAN CLONING.

ADMINISTRATORS AT
SNAILVILLE SCHOOL LAMENT
THE SPEED OF CHANGE.

A NEW TWIST ON SCHOOL BUSSING.

MR. MOODY TRIES A NEW TECHNIQUE
AFTER GETTING LOST AT A NATIONAL
EDUCATION CONFERENCE AND SPENDING
A WEEK AT A USED CAR SALES SEMINAR.

HAROLD GETS TO USE NEW MAPPING SOFTWARE TO GIVE ELLEN A GEOGRAPHY LESSON IN INCLUSIVE EDUCATION.

AS A LAST RESORT, SCHOOL STAFF
FOUND A WAY TO HELP MR. MOODY GET
UP ON THE RIGHT SIDE OF THE BED.

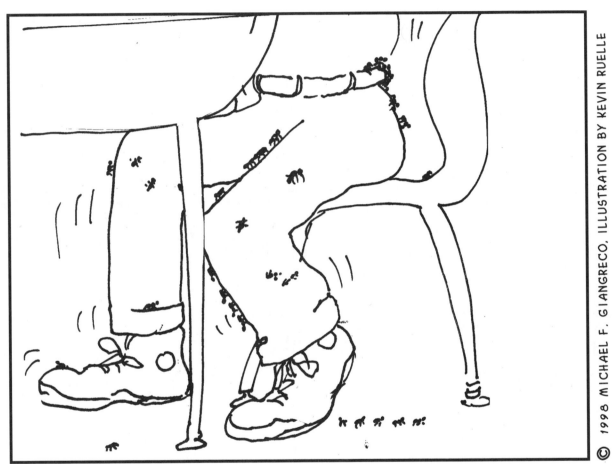

AFTER A HASTY SPECIAL EDUCATION
PLACEMENT FOR BEHAVIOR PROBLEMS,
SCHOOL OFFICIALS WERE EMBARRASSED
TO LEARN THAT MARTY REALLY DID HAVE
ANTS IN HIS PANTS.

CONTINUALLY CONFUSED BY EVER-CHANGING
DISABILITY LABELS, MR. MOODY IS ANNOYED
WHEN HE REALIZES THE 5 STUDENTS BORN ON
APRIL 1ST HAVE TO BE DECLASSIFIED.

MR. CRUSTY WELCOMES FRED TO THE
LOBSTERVILLE SPECIAL EDUCATION
CENTER WHERE THEIR MOTTO IS
"YOU CAN GET IN, BUT YOU CAN'T GET OUT!"

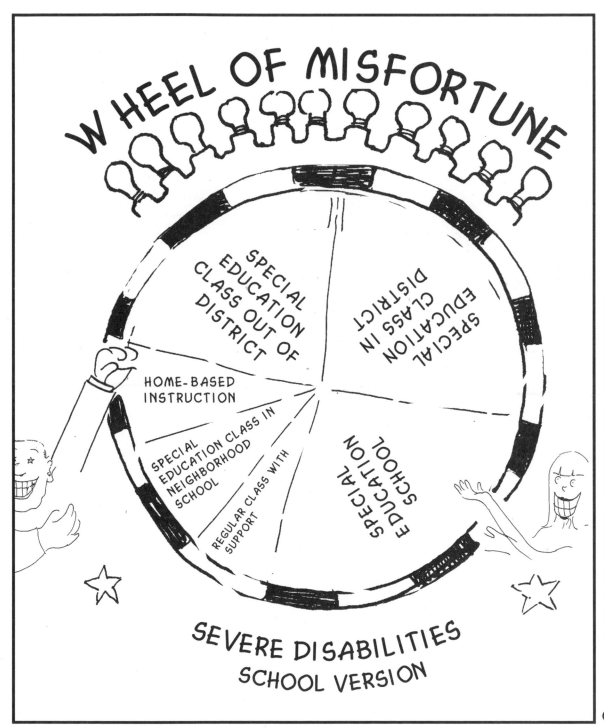

21

SPACE JAM

SPACE MAKER

MR. MOODY DISPLAYS HIS
FLAIR FOR THE DRAMATIC.

THE AMAZING INCLUSIVE EDUCATION
TEACHER TRANSFORMATION MACHINE

FRANK LEARNS THAT INCLUSION DOESN'T
HAVE TO BE ROCKET SCIENCE.

IN THE MARRIAGE OF GENERAL AND
SPECIAL EDUCATION, BOTH PARTIES AGREE
TO LEAVE THEIR BAGGAGE AT THE DOOR.

© 1998 MICHAEL F GIANGRECO. ILLUSTRATION BY KEVIN RUELLE
PEYTRAL PUBLICATIONS, INC. 952-949-8707   www.peytral.com

ISLAND IN THE MAINSTREAM

MRS. JONES AND MRS. COOPER ARE
STILL TRYING TO FIGURE OUT WHY FRED
DOESN'T FEEL LIKE PART OF THE CLASS.

INCLUSIVE EDUCATION:
DOING IT WRONG DOESN'T MAKE IT WRONG.

AFTER BEING SOLD A "BILL OF GOODS",
MRS. MARTIN IS SURPRISED TO LEARN
IT'S DEFECTIVE.

INCLUSIVE EDUCATION
BECOMES A MOOT POINT

INCLUSION MISHAP #9: DUE TO A FAULTY INTERCOM, MRS. SNIPPETT THOUGHT THE PRINCIPAL SAID, "YOU HAVE A NEW STUDENT COMING TO YOUR CLASSROOM - HE HAS DISABILITIES. DO YOUR BEST TO *ELUDE* HIM."

MRS. FINE
WONDERS
IF IT'S
TOO LATE
TO REQUEST
A LARGER
CLASSROOM.

INSPIRED BY MARY BETH DOYLE

© 1998 MICHAEL F. GIANGRECO. ILLUSTRATION BY KEVIN RUELLE
PEYTRAL PUBLICATIONS, INC. 952-949-8707   www.peytral.com

THE ABC'S OF INCLUSION

AFTER SEVERAL ATTEMPTS, FRED BEGINS
TO REALIZE THAT COOKBOOK RECIPES
FOR INCLUSION JUST DON'T WORK.

PRINCIPAL JONES FAILS TO RECOGNIZE THE CONTRADICTION IN TERMS.

JASON'S MOTHER HAS A CLOSE ENCOUNTER WITH THE OLD SAYING: "THE ONLY THING WORSE THAN NOT GETTING WHAT YOU WANT IS GETTING WHAT YOU WANT."

SPECIAL EDUCATION STUDENTS TURN TO
GAMBLING TO AVOID THE BOREDOM OF
AGE-INAPPROPRIATE ACTIVITIES.

SOMETIMES HAVING SO MANY VISITORS
MAKES MRS. GROUPER FEEL LIKE SHE'S IN
A FISH BOWL.

AFTER HAVING SUCCESSFULLY TAUGHT
STUDENTS WITH A WIDE RANGE OF
CHARACTERISTICS, MS. MILLER DECIDED
TO ADJUST HER WARDROBE TO MATCH
HER TEACHING CONFIDENCE.

MRS. JONES EXPLAINS HER
SECRET TO NEVER GETTING
BENT OUT OF SHAPE.

AFTER RULING OUT A MEDICAL REASON,
BOBBY SUE'S PARENTS COME TO THE
CONCLUSION THAT THERE'S JUST A LOT
MORE TO BE AWAKE FOR IN REGULAR CLASS.

PRINCIPAL MOODY INTRODUCES THE
SCHOOL DISTRICT'S NEW ADVOCATE TO
DEFEND EXCLUSION.

THE BAR ASSOCIATION PROPOSES A
AMENDMENT TO IDEA REQUIRING THAT
LAWYERS BE PART OF EVERY
CHILD'S IEP TEAM.

MRS. HOPE FOUND THAT SOME OF HER BEST INSTRUCTORS WERE STILL IN SECOND GRADE.

PEERS
RESORT
TO
SUBVERSIVE
TACTICS

MYSTERIES OF FRIENDSHIP.

LITTLE LEAGUE TEAMMATES LEARN THERE
ARE MANY WAYS TO CONTRIBUTE.

MARC GIVES
NEW MEANING
TO DRAWING
A LINE IN THE
SAND.

FRIENDS APPLY LESSONS OF
CREATIVE PROBLEM SOLVING TO
EVERY DAY LIFE.

PEG DOESN'T KNOW THAT THE KIDS WITH DISABILITIES IN HER OLD DISTRICT WERE SENT TO SPECIAL EDUCATION SCHOOLS.

DESPITE THE BIO-ETHICAL CONTROVERSIES
MAGGIE FAVORS HUMAN CLONING.

THIS IS COLLABORATIVE TEAMWORK

THIS IS COLLABORATIVE TEAMWORK ON STEROIDS.

OUTNUMBERED?

MARTY CONTINUES TO THINK OF HIMSELF
AS A TEAM OF ONE.

HERB AND SALLY ADD THE ELUSIVE
"COLLABORATIVE TEAM" TO THEIR
LIFE LIST OF RARE
AND ENDANGERED SPECIES.

ADVENTURES IN ZIPPING
ZONE OF PROXIMAL CONFUSION

FRED EXPRESSES CONCERN AFTER TEAM
MEMBERS AGREE TO ALL PULL IN
DIFFERENT DIRECTIONS.

AFTER A UNIDIRECTIONAL EXPERIENCE
WITH ROLE RELEASE, HENRY FEELS LIKE
HE IS LEFT HOLDING THE BAG.

SEVERELY DYSFUNCTIONAL TEAM

HARVEY CONTINUES TO ASK THE WRONG
QUESTION IN A ROOM FULL OF HELPERS.

SOMETIMES EVEN
"VOTING REGULARITIES"
CAN BE PROBLEMATIC.

AFTER MONTHS OF PUBLIC AGREEMENT
AND PRIVATE DISAGREEMENT, THE
TEAM DECIDES TO FIND OUT WHAT
EVERYONE IS THINKING.

HAVING SUFFERED THROUGH EXCESSIVE
EXPOSURE TO PROFESSIONALS, PARENTS
LOOK FOR FUN WAYS OF COPING.

STAIR WARS

FREDDIE IS NOT AMUSED BY HIS PHYSICAL THERAPIST'S CHOICE OF HALLOWEEN COSTUME.

BEING UNFAMILIAR WITH THERAPEUTIC
TECHNIQUES, KELSEY FEARS HER CLASSMATE
MIGHT BE ON THE RECEIVING END OF A
KNEE-DROP OR A BODY SLAM.

HARRY PERSISTS IN PUTTING
SUPPORT SERVICES BEFORE
EDUCATIONAL GOALS AND PLACEMENT.

ONLY IN A PHYSICAL
THERAPIST'S DREAM.

THE #1 SIGN A TEACHER DOES NOT FIND A CONSULTANT'S INPUT SUPPORTIVE:

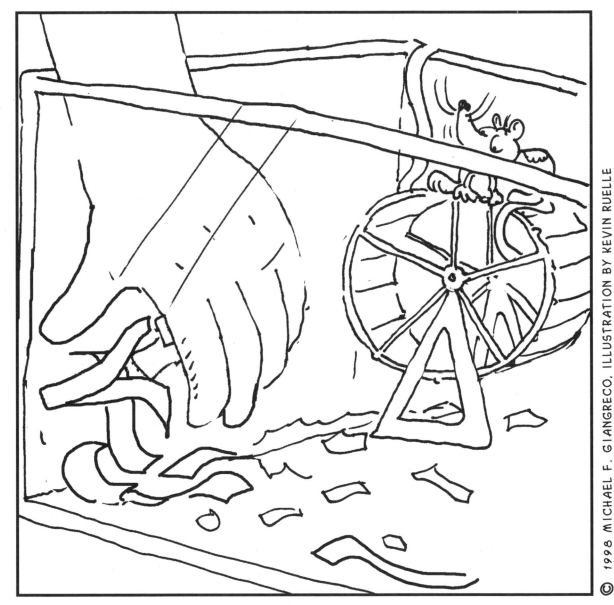

CONSULTANT'S REPORT IS FOUND SHREDDED AS BEDDING FOR THE CLASSROOM HAMSTER.

MATCHING SUPPORTS TO NEEDS
CONTINUES TO BE AN ELUSIVE
EXPERIENCE FOR HARRY.

IN THE CADAVER LAB, PHYSICAL THERAPY
AND SCHOOL PSYCHOLOGY STUDENTS
WORK TOGETHER IN AN EXPERIMENTAL
INTERDISCIPLINARY TRAINING PROGRAM.

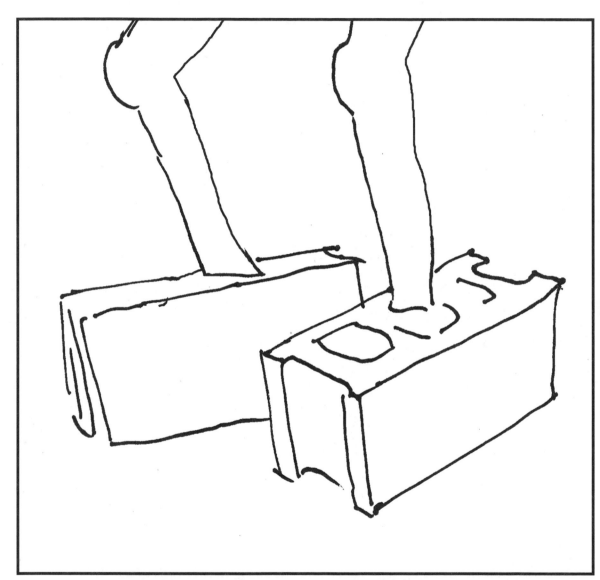

A FORMER GANGSTER TURNED THERAPIST
RELIES ON OLD SKILLS IN DEVELOPING HIS
EXPERIMENTAL "CEMENT SHOE THERAPY."

DESPITE THE BIO-ETHICAL CONTROVERSIES MAGGIE FAVORS HUMAN CLONING.

GUARDIAN ANGEL

SUPER-MAGNET

STUCK LIKE GLUE

HOVERCRAFT

HELPING OR HOVERING?

DESPITE HAVING A MASTER'S AND 18 YEARS OF EXPERIENCE, MRS. SNIPPETT TRIES TO CONVINCE MR. MOODY THAT THE STUDENT WITH DISABILITIES IN HER CLASS WOULD BE BETTER SERVED BY AN ASSISTANT WITH NO EXPERIENCE.

AFTER A GRUELING MEETING,
THE STAFF DECIDES TO LET
MRS. BROWN KEEP HER NAME.

SECOND GRADE STUDENTS PONDER
ONE OF THE GREAT MYSTERIES OF
HILLVIEW SCHOOL.

SCHOOL LUNCH ATROCITIES

JOEY NOTICED A MYSTERIOUS FORCE FIELD
AROUND HIS ASSISTANT THAT CHILDREN
COULD NOT BREAK THROUGH.

AFTER ONLY TWO MONTHS AS A TEACHER
ASSISTANT, GLADYS FINDS HER SPELLING
HAS IMPROVED, MATH SKILLS ARE HONED,
AND SHE HAS DISCOVERED SHE HAS
ARTISTIC ABILITY.

FRED'S INSTRUCTIONAL ASSISTANT
MAKES SURE SHE AND FRED ARE
POSITIONED CLOSE TO AN EXIT TO MAKE
ANY ESCAPE ATTEMPTS LESS
CONSPICUOUS.

UNINTENDED
DISTRACTIONS

THE INSTRUCTIONAL ASSISTANT
ASSIGNED TO PAT EXPERIENCES ONGOING
GENDER CONFUSION.

THE PROFESSIONAL STAFF RESORT TO
USING PROPS JUST SO THE TEACHER
ASSISTANT IS CLEAR THEY ARE
PASSING THE BUCK.

UNFORTUNATELY, THE TEACHER
ASSISTANT'S BURNING QUESTIONS KEPT
SPONTANEOUSLY COMBUSTING BEFORE
THEY COULD BE ANSWERED.

MR. GREEN PREPARES FOR HIS
CHILD'S IEP MEETING

AFTER YEARS OF PLAYING CAT AND MOUSE TO DEVELOP AN IEP, CASEY'S MOTHER LONGS FOR A CHANCE TO BE THE CAT FOR ONCE!

RODNEY IS CAUGHT WITH HIS PANTS DOWN -
WRITING IEP GOALS AND OBJECTIVES
WITHOUT FAMILY INPUT.

DAVID TRANSLATES FOR HANK WHO IS
JUST LEARNING TO SPEAK JARGONESE AS
A SECOND LANGUAGE.

SPECIAL ED COORDINATOR,
MR. CROSSWAY, HAS WATCHED
TOO MANY OLD RE-RUNS OF
SATURDAY NIGHT LIVE.

IS BIGGER BETTER?

FRED FINDS FILLING FILE CABINETS A
STRANGELY FULFILLING PART OF HIS JOB.

INDIVIDUALIZED EDUCATION:
MRS. SMITHFIELD FAILS TO NOTICE
THE CONTRADICTION.

FRANK ELEVATES VAGUENESS
TO AN ART FORM.

MISS PLEPPER WAS ABSENT FOR THE INSERVICE
ON CULTURAL AND LINGUISTIC DIVERSITY.

x

TRANSFORM YOUR SEPARATE, DISJOINTED, DISCIPLINE-SPECIFIC, UNCOORDINATED GOALS INTO A "TEAM IEP."

SPECIAL EDUCATION COORDINATOR, MR. PETERS, USES A LOW-TECH SOLUTION TO AVOID CONFRONTATIONS AND THREATS OF DUE-PROCESS HEARINGS.

THE MOST RECENT COMPUTERIZED IEP'S
ARE TOO CUT AND DRIED.

MURRAY HAS SPENT TOO MANY YEARS WITH STUDENTS WHO LEARN REGARDLESS OF WHAT THE TEACHER DOES.

DESPITE THE BIO-ETHICAL CONTROVERSIES MAGGIE FAVORS HUMAN CLONING.

ELLEN THINKS "SPEAKING LOUDLY"
IS A FORM OF
SPECIALIZED INSTRUCTION.

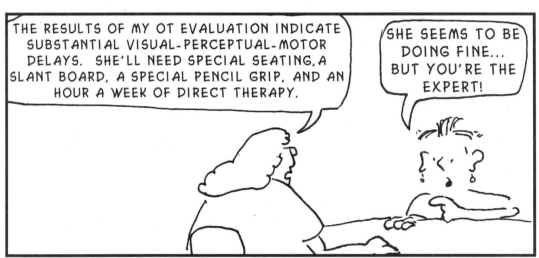

MRS. BAKER QUESTIONS HER 20 YEARS OF EXPERIENCE AS A SECOND GRADE TEACHER AND SUCCUMBS TO THE AWESOME POWER OF TEST RESULTS.

MRS. WALKER LEARNS THE HARD WAY
THAT SOMETIMES 80% CORRECT JUST
ISN'T GOOD ENOUGH.

RODNEY LEARNS NOT TO MAKE
A MOVE UNTIL HE IS TOLD.

AFTER WEEKS OF INSTRUCTION, SUSIE
LEARNS THAT "CUP" MEANS ANYTHING
IN THE TOP RIGHT CORNER.

MR. GREEN'S STUDENTS EXPERIENCE
"CUE CONFUSION."

PATTY'S TEACHER RETURNED THE BOOK
ON APPLIED BEHAVIOR ANALYSIS BEFORE
HE HAD A CHANCE TO READ THE CHAPTER
ON FADING PHYSICAL PROMPTS.

CHARLOTTE AND MAGGIE CONSIDER
COMING OUT OF THE CLOSET ABOUT
THEIR GRAPHING TENDENCIES.

AFTER SPENDING *10* MINUTES EACH
AFTERNOON IN FRONT OF A FULL-LENGTH
MIRROR, ALAN STILL ISN'T SURE WHY
SELF-REFLECTION IS SO IMPORTANT TO
GOOD TEACHING.

LARRY LEARNS THE HARD WAY THAT
SCHOOL AND THE REAL WORLD DON'T
ALWAYS SEE SUCCESS THE SAME WAY.

Additional Cartoon Books!

Written by Michael F. Giangreco and Illustrated by Kevin Ruelle

With wit, humor and profound one-liners, Michael Giangreco and Kevin Ruelle will transform your thinking as you take a lighter look at the often comical and occasionally harsh truth in the ever-changing field of special education.

These inspiring cartoon books, shed light onto the real-life situations frequently encountered by those involved with the special education system. Each of the following publications include a collection of 100+ carefully crafted cartoons that will inspire and entertain, while providing a scrupulous look into the absurdities and realities of virtually all areas of special education.

Each publication covers a wide variety of topics: inclusive education, self-advocacy, paraprofessionals, families, positive behavior support, support services, least restrictive environment, collaboration, individual education plans, disability labeling, and standards are only a few.

These cartoons are exceptional staff development tools as the full-page cartoons may be reproduced as transparencies directly from the book! These exceptional cartoons will help inform, encourage dialogue, spur action to improve education, and reduce stress through humor.

Ants in His Pants:
Absurdities and Realities of Special Education
P101 / $19.95 / 1998 Release

Flying by the Seat of Your Pants:
More Absurdities and Realities of Special Education
P 102 / $19.95 / 1999 Release

Teaching Old Logs New Tricks:
More Absurdities and Realities of Education
P 103 / $19.95 / 2000 Release

Additional Books!

Choosing Outcomes and Accommodations for Children (COACH)-A Guide to Educational Planning for Students with Disabilities
Michael F. Giangreco, Ph.D., Chigee J. Cloninger, Ph.D., & Virginia Salce Iverson, M.Ed.

Using the established and field-tested methods of COACH, educators, related services providers, and school administrators can collaborate with families to develop a meaningful IEP for each student. This second edition offers redesigned forms, more detailed explanations, explicit instructions, helpful hints for each step, and tabs and icons to make information easy to find. Also in this edition: an updated family interview, cross-cultural adaptations, forms for developing IEP goals and objectives, and new materials for lesson planning and program evaluation.

The established and field-tested methods of this practical edition make it easy for general and special educators, related service providers, school administrators, and parents to collaborate and work toward developing a meaningful IEP for each student. Additional COACH Student Record Forms may be purchased separately.

B 104 / Second edition of COACH / 400 pages / $39.95
B 104 F / 3 Packages of Student Record Forms / 72 pgs each / $23.95

Vermont Interdependent Services Team Approach (VISTA) A Guide to Coordinating Education Support Services
Michael F. Giangreco, Ph.D.

VISTA provides a practical, step-by-step framework that enables teams to make support services decisions using a collaborative approach. By progressing through the 10 straightforward guidelines of the VISTA process, IEP team members will learn to: establish the components of an educational plan; determine the educational necessity of support services; fulfill the related services provisions of IDEA; use natural supports appropriately; and foster the acquisition of functional skills.

Real-life examples show how this flexible process can support students with a range of characteristics, and reproducible forms ease the implementation of VISTA. Practical, methodical, and detailed, VISTA enables educators, administrators, support service providers, family members, and other team members to work together more efficiently to expand students' educational opportunities. B103 / VISTA / 176 pgs / $27.95

Quick-Guides to Inclusion
Edited by Michael F. Giangreco, Ph.D.

Perfect for busy educators, these two user-friendly books offer brief, to-the-point advice for improving inclusion skills. Each spiral bound, photocopiable handbook consists of five "Quick-Guides" devoted to a relevant topic, offering easy-to-follow ideas, tips, examples, and suggestions that teachers, administrators, and related services personnel can put to use immediately. Equally suitable as entry-level guides or as concise summaries of practices for seasoned professionals, these classroom tools help make inclusion work in any school!

Quick-Guides to Inclusion - Ideas for Educating Students with Disabilities

The first guide covers the following topics: including students with disabilities in the classroom; building partnerships with parents; creating partnerships with paraprofessionals; getting the most out of support services; and creating positive behavioral supports. B 100 / 160 pgs / spiral bound / $23.95

Quick-Guides to Inclusion 2 - Ideas for Educating Students with Disabilities

The second book covers the following topics: adapting the curriculum; instructional strategies; communication systems in the classroom; administration in inclusive schools; and transition from school to adult life.
B 101 / 160 pgs / spiral bound / $23.95

Quick-Guides to Inclusion 3 - Available in 2001

The third book in this series will be available in 2001. Please call Peytral Publications, Inc. for an update on this title.

Order the Set and Save!
B010 / Set of 2 / Quick Guide and Quick Guide 2 / $43.95

Peytral Publications, Inc. is a publisher and distributor books and staff development videos that promote Success for All Learners.

If you have questions, would like to request a catalog, or place an order, please contact *Peytral Publications, Inc.* We will be happy to help you.

Peytral Publications, Inc.
PO Box 1162
Minnetonka, MN   55345

Toll Free Orders: 1-877-PEYTRAL (877-739-8725)
Questions: (952) 949-8707
Fax: 952.906.9777

Or visit us online at:
www.peytral.com